The World
of Water

The World of Water

Exploring the Sacramento Delta

ERLE STANLEY GARDNER

William Morrow & Company
New York 1965

**Other Books of Travel and Adventure
by Erle Stanley Gardner**

THE LAND OF SHORTER SHADOWS
NEIGHBORHOOD FRONTIERS
HUNTING THE DESERT WHALE
HOVERING OVER BAJA
THE HIDDEN HEART OF BAJA
THE DESERT IS YOURS

Contents

Color photographs appear after page 128

List of Illustrations

The World of Water

The World of Water

Early morning reflections shattered by wake of the boat.

Acknowledgment

The photographs in this book were taken for the most part by the author, with the assistance of Jean Bethell, Sam Hicks, and Dick DeShazer.

An attempt was made to get photographs which would illustrate the story wherever possible and give the reader an idea of what the country is like and what living in a house cruiser is like.

To that end, we all carried cameras and took pictures from time to time and place to place. My associates generously placed their pictures at my disposal, and I freely selected those which suited my purpose.

I am tremendously grateful to the DeShazers — both Dick and Moyne — for their co-operation. They love the Delta country, they love boats, they are ideal camping companions, and they have gone to a lot of trouble to help me get the material I wanted.

The World of Water

My staff has been with me for many years on many an adventure and, while I take their co-operation for granted, it is not unfitting at this time to make a public acknowledgment of their faithful and unfailing efficiency and loyalty.

ERLE STANLEY GARDNER

A world of water and boats.

Foreword

This book deals with boats and water and with the Sacramento Delta country of California where the San Joaquin, the North and South Forks of the Mokelumne River and the Sacramento River all join in forming an incredible thousand miles of inland waterways.

Comparatively few people know about this boating paradise.

Most of those who do know about it have boats. The people who live there are boat-conscious. Boats are owned, boats are sold and boats are rented. It is a world of its own, a world of boats, a place where little one-family restaurants serve home-cooked meals to customers who tie up their boats at guest docks hospitably maintained for the purpose.

Yet this fabulous Delta country is typical of many other places in the United States, places which are beginning to come into their own as people discover The World of Water.

The World
of Water

Boats streak over the water.

CHAPTER **1**

A Gypsy Existence

Now that weekend automobile traffic is all but bumper to bumper, and people who have laboriously journeyed to the national forests find that all the camping places are filled to overflowing, there is a growing tendency to take to the water.

There are various ways of traveling on water, and various boats have been designed for each type of travel.

The water skier has a powerful, sleek boat which gets into action rapidly. The here-to-there water travelers have hot rods which streak over the water, and the affluent professional man has his luxurious cruiser.

The houseboat crowd isn't in a hurry to get from here to there because once they get aboard the houseboat and cast loose the moorings they are there.

Houseboating consists primarily of camping on water, living a gypsy existence, sitting back and enjoying the beauties of nature and the relaxation of utter tranquility.

Houseboat living is probably one of the *few* forms of camping which has almost *no* handicaps.

17

Luxurious cruisers abound.

Houseboating means camping on the water.

Living a gypsy existence.

Virtually everyone likes to camp, but all campers know the handicaps inherent in sleeping out of doors. These include ants in the syrup, sand in the food, dew on the bed or the tent, wet canvas to roll up in the morning, the fear of occasional showers at night and the job of packing and unpacking.

There was a time when the house trailer was the acme of perfection in the field of camping.

I have always loved camping, and was one of the pioneers with house trailers. I experimented with just about everything. Nearly all of these trailers were wonderful. But in the early days we had problems — built-in problems.

Manufacturers had failed to consider the problem of insulation. On a cold, damp night the inside of the trailer would fill up with moist air. A gasoline heating stove would be used to warm the inside of the trailer. As the interior air became warm, it would strike against cold walls and condense into moisture. Trickles of water would run down from this con-

19

The author, a confirmed trailorite, and Jean Bethell.

densation, form in puddles on the floor and coat everything in the trailer with beads of moisture.

Yet those were the beautiful days of trailering. A man could pull off at the side of the road just about anywhere and spend a day or two days, if he wanted. He could go to the desert in the winter, find a side road, run down it for a mile and establish a more or less permanent residence.

Then, as trailers began to be perfected, sheer numbers created a problem. People objected to trailerites stopping by the roadside on private property. Trailer camps were established — and the early trailer camp left much to be desired. With public lavatories, the morning procession was like having a sumptuously appointed room in a boardinghouse where there was only one bathroom at the end of a very long hall.

Again came improvement as individual plumbing facilities were installed in trailers, and trailer parks provided indi-

Manufacturers have solved the problems of shallow draft and high wind resistance.

The bow is pointed, the hull is streamlined.

Camping in its most ideal form.

vidual parking spaces connected with running water and sewage disposal, and a main social hall with television and card tables. These trailer parks became small cities with a delightfully informal social life, as more and more people took to trailer life. The modern trailer is a satisfying place to live.

Originally the houseboat was pretty much a homemade affair. But manufacturers rapidly began to solve the problems inherent in a boat of shallow draft and high wind resistance.

Now a relatively new development is taking place: the house cruiser.

The traditional houseboat has a blunt, scowlike bow and generally is somewhat underpowered for the simple reason that more power would give the contraption very little more speed. Recently this problem has been solved, at least in part, by putting the houseboat on catamaran-type streamlined floats.

22

There are fish to be had for the taking.

The World of Water

The house cruiser, however, and more particularly the recent ones with steel hulls, are just about ideal in combining camping, cruising, fishing, relaxing and just plain loafing.

Because the bow is pointed and the hull is streamlined, it is possible to use more power and get more speed. With more power, the effects of wind resistance and currents can be largely controlled. The modern house cruiser is a very maneuverable unit.

And, of course, the advantages of a houseboat are such that one enjoys camping in its most ideal form.

In a suitable waterway one can anchor or tie up whenever one pleases. There are fish to be had for the taking, pots and pans are stored within easy reach of a gas or electric range. The refinements create a sense of carefree luxury which is almost unknown in any other form of existence. The beds are

One can anchor or tie up wherever one pleases.

One hour later the fish may be biting.

Houseboats at Terminous.

conducive to deep sleep. Clothes closets provide hangers for such additional clothes as may be needed either for shore trips or yachting.

If one wants to fish, there is no need to set the alarm clock, get up before daylight, drive for a couple of hours and then find a fishing spot. On a houseboat one simply rolls out of bed, tosses out a line and by the time the coffee is percolating he knows whether or not the fish are biting.

If they aren't, he needs only to dunk a doughnut in the coffee, turn on the radio and go back to bed.

An hour later the fish may be biting.

CHAPTER **2**

The Mainstays of My Fleet

My friend Richard DeShazer is a houseboat enthusiast. It was, therefore, only natural that he should begin to supplement his yacht brokerage business with houseboats, and soon the tail began wagging the dog.

Having been a pioneer customer in the automotive trailer business, I became interested in the possibilities of house cruisers.

I purchased a 1963 "River Queen" from DeShazer at Bethel Island, used it rather briefly and was enthusiastic about it — until the new models came in, models which featured more storage space, more power, twin engines, more flexibility of control and, of course, more speed.

So I traded in the single-engine 1963 model and bought a 1964 River Queen.

It soon became apparent, however, that I needed additional space if I was going to work while cruising and accommodate some of the friends, editors and publishers who came

Dick DeShazer, distributor in the west for the Whit-Craft and the River Queen, is a houseboat enthusiast.

Whit-Craft heading upstream.

to visit me from time to time, and when I saw the compact "Whit-Craft," with its quick maneuverability, I purchased one to use with the River Queen.

There is, incidentally, something of a story connected with the design of the Whit-Craft; a story in which Dick DeShazer has a part.

DeShazer was, at one time, in the boat-building and boat-designing business. At that time he was trying to work out the most efficient small boat which could possibly be designed.

He and his partner developed a model so carefully that they virtually reached the ultimate in perfection. As Dick explained it to me, changing the design of that boat by whittling off so much as the thickness of a pencil mark in one of the key parts would materially affect the efficiency of its performance.

As soon as I saw the Whit-Craft I wanted one.

The Whit-Craft has three shearwater prows.

Dick DeShazer, the author, and a denizen of the deep.

The Whit-Craft makes an ideal second boat.

Apparently this was a remarkable boat. It couldn't be made to capsize even when turned at its highest speed. Nor would it pound or "porpoise" — the jumping action which characterizes so many small boats at high speed.

In short, Dick knows boats, loves boats and loves to design boats.

When Dick saw the first Whit-Craft, which at that time had two shear-water prows, giving the boat a sort of catamaran design, he felt that its performance would be improved if a third, middle shear-water were placed in the center. He had a series of talks with Richard Whittaker, who designed and manufactured the Whit-Craft. Whittaker, knowing Dick DeShazer's reputation, started experimenting, and finally decided to use a hull which has the three shear-water prows, a large one in the center and one on each side.

Now I am not familiar enough with boats to know how these things affect the performance, but I do know that once

We use the Valco for running errands.

he got this design perfected Whittaker telephoned Dick with great jubilation and told him that he had a craft that just walked away from anything else in its class. DeShazer, with characteristic decision, said, "Start shipping them to me. I'm your West Coast distributor."

That was how it happened that we started out on two houseboats. The 1964 River Queen, which is thirty-eight feet long and weighs about eight tons, is equipped with an air conditioning system, generator, electric kitchen, hot and cold running water under pressure, and all the gadgets of a deluxe apartment.

The Whit-Craft, lighter, smaller, remarkably easy to handle and efficiently designed, made an ideal second boat — one that could be used for guests over a weekend or, on occasion, one that could be used for men alone while the River Queen housed the feminine members of the party and became the culinary headquarters.

33

A script comes in and is read . . .

These house cruisers were the mainstays of my fleet, so to speak.

However, I also had need for smaller fast boats for errands, supplies and for telephones whenever privacy was required.

Our house cruisers had radio telephones so we could keep in touch with one another, and if necessary call on long distance. However, since I have some rather complicated business affairs and, most important of all, a weekly, hour-long television show, it was necessary that I have frequent contacts with my main office in Temecula and with the television studio in Hollywood where the conversations would be private.

So with my fleet of smaller boats, when I wanted to keep the house cruisers tied up, I could streak in to the nearest telephone without any loss of time. Because of incoming scripts and mail I fixed up a field office with secretaries,

34

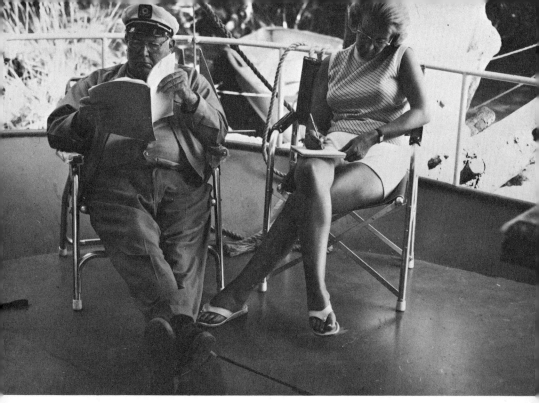

Millie Conarroe takes notes . . .

. . . and transcribes them for rush mailing to Hollywood.

The Valco is fine for fishing, too.

portable typewriters and dictating machines. I even had a small transistor-powered television set.

These chains to the business world sound formidable and at times they were, but at other times the chains were agreeably slack. The point is that my transportation needs were far in excess of those of the average yachtsman.

We had a small double-ended dinghy, a fourteen-foot "Valco," of sturdy aluminum, powered with an eighteen-horsepower Johnson outboard, a nineteen-foot heavy-duty "Smithcraft," powered with twin Johnson outboards and a twenty-three-foot "Trojan" express cruiser powered with a Ford "Interceptor."

These boats could go very fast indeed, and because we had plenty of transportation there was always a boat available for photography, fishing, errand running or for exploration in strange waters whenever anyone wanted to go.

36

The Mainstays of My Fleet

It was my idea that we explore the hundreds of miles of sloughs running up through the Delta country and make a leisurely survey of the possibilities of camping in house cruisers.

The Sacramento Delta country should be more fully explained. All of the inland waters are subject to rise and fall inasmuch as tides from the San Francisco Bay area raise and lower the water, but the water itself in the Delta region is fresh.

Counting the Sacramento River — as far north as it is practical for a small boat to navigate — and the miles of so-called sloughs, there are more than a thousand miles of winding waterways, running for the most part between levees.

These waters include some of the best fishing in the world. It is possible to catch black bass, catfish, blue gill, sturgeon

Our house cruisers in camp.

It was my idea to explore the hundreds of miles of sloughs.

and several other varieties, but the country is chiefly noted for its striped bass.

During the "runs" of striped bass those gamy fish are literally hauled in by the ton on the hooks and lines of hundreds of ardent fishing enthusiasts.

These fish can be taken by anglers who use an almost infinite variety of boats, from the expensive yacht equipped with twin diesels to the small outboard motor-powered boat which is carried on an auto trailer — some of them are carried on car tops — and there are rental boats available at many of the marinas.

Our fourteen-foot Valco can be carried on the top of a camper, or transported by trailer to whatever place is most convenient for launching. It is a sturdy, small craft, so perfectly constructed that it seems to fairly dart over the water, just skimming the surface.

The Smithcraft can also be transported by trailer. It is

The author studies a map of the Inland Waterways of the Delta.

A luxurious home afloat.

much heavier than the Valco although both are of aluminum alloy. The Smithcraft was designed for rough water in the Gulf of California and is tremendously strong. Its twin motors send it over the water at something above twenty miles an hour.

The Trojan express cruiser is very fast, can do well over thirty miles an hour and is capable of handling just about any problem of transportation we would ask. Several people can be very comfortable on it. It has sleeping space for two people in the enclosed cabin, ample space for fishing, a "head," an alcohol stove and a small stainless steel sink.

Any of these boats are fine for fishing for striped bass, the fish for which the Delta district is famous.

And there are of course dozens, probably hundreds, of other makes of boats — one for every purse, one for every possible use. Just as we have different makes and models of

40

Boats in Bethel Island dock.

Cruiser approaching.

Setting forth in the Valco.

automobiles, so do we have different makes and models of boats.

I am at a point in life where I prefer the relatively quiet sport of fishing for catfish and pan-fish in the eddies and in secluded bends where I can be by myself.

All of which helps explain my enthusiasm for house cruisers.

These boats, with their steel hulls, their pointed bows reinforced with heavy steel beams, give them speed, stability and maneuverability and, at the same time, great strength. You can put one of these boats ashore where you wouldn't dare to venture with one of the more conventional and less ruggedly constructed cruisers.

Before we started on our first house-cruiser trip, I explained to Dick what I wanted.

I wanted to go where we could tie up boats in the shade of trees, where we could be completely undisturbed, where we

Fishing for catfish.

Jean Bethell and Moyne DeShazer breakfast on the bow of the River Queen.

could work as occasion required, knock off work and catch catfish when we wanted, sit out on deck in the long, lazy afternoons, watching the fish jumping, listening to the birds, completely free from care. Then when night fell, we could have all the cooking facilities that would be found in an expensive apartment house, have a dinner on the deck or in the dining compartment, and afterwards sink into deep, blissful slumber, undisturbed by the myriad noises of civilization.

Not only did I make this sound so attractive to Dick that he sold me the house cruisers with which to make my dream come true, but after I purchased the '64 Whit-Craft and River Queen, Dick and his wife, Moyne, decided to come along with us and show me some of the places where I could find exactly what I was looking for.

So we started out with our fleet of boats, headed up Sand Mound Slough with nothing in mind except achieving the one goal which I had for the trip—a carefree existence.

There was a time when the words "carefree existence" were very much a part of our language. One seldom hears them any more. The multiple tensions of civilization have conspired to make these words more or less meaningless, and it is seldom that a situation arises where they can truthfully be used.

This is not true in the boating world, however; here there is still a carefree existence to be had, particularly in the Delta region.

We decided to take the two house cruisers, the Smithcraft and the Trojan, under their own power. Later, when we had made a semi-permanent camp, we would get the fourteen-foot Valco and "trailer" it up to the nearest convenient launching ramp.

I wanted to be sure that we had enough boats so everyone could fish, photograph or explore whenever the spirit moved. If we were going to live an ideal existence, there

Millie Conarroe, Moyne DeShazer and Jean Bethell relax while we take on gasoline.

was no need to put up with inconveniences or ration transportation.

Both house cruisers are powered with the famous Ford Interceptor engines and have the inboard-outboard drive, a combination which has proved so efficient it has virtually changed the whole concept of houseboating.

The actual draft of these boats is measured in inches rather than feet, but they have sufficient power and maneuverability so that wind resistance, which had been the bugaboo of earlier houseboating, is now a relatively negligible factor.

All in all we had a perfect setup for the carefree existence I was contemplating. I could handle what work simply had to be done, and for the rest I could explore the Delta waterways.

CHAPTER **3**

From Striped Bass to Catfish

For some years the Delta country had exerted a fascination upon me. For years I had been intending really to explore it, but up to the time I started out with my assortment of boats I had made only a few short trips, intending, at least for the record, to fish for striped bass.

Almost without exception these trips never became striped bass fishing expeditions. We would start out, head for the swifter water, where the better striped bass fishing exists, but on the way I would see an eddy which looked like promising catfish grounds and I would say, "Sam, let's swing over there and just drop our lines for a few minutes to see if there are any catfish. If there are, we can remember it for future reference."

The Sam I was addressing is Sam Hicks, who has been my companion for years on almost all my expeditions, either in the desert searching for adventure or lost mines or down in Baja California exploring by Pak-Jak, Burrito and helicopter;

46

Sam Hicks.

getting into country where no tourist has ever penetrated, and more recently Sam has learned to pilot the house cruisers.

Sam is naturally adaptable, one of those thoroughly competent individuals who can adjust himself to just about any situation. He has chain-lightning reactions, and can learn anything in a short period of time.

Not only has he taken up photography and writing, but he has sold quite a bit of material to magazines. In addition to being a wonderful companion, Sam is a resourceful, highly skilled woodsman and an expert camper.

Until recently Sam rather snorted at the idea of fishing because he is primarily a hunter. But the house cruisers and the Delta country have exerted their spell, and now Sam has become quite expert as a fisherman. For a while he pretended he was just doing something to kill time while we

Sam has become quite expert as a fisherman.

Jean Bethell has been my chief secretary for many years.

were anchored or tied up, but now he can no longer conceal his interest.

Our first catfishing expeditions were mostly on the 1963 River Queen or the Trojan and were for a few hours at a time, usually in the late afternoon.

While I am free to do a good deal of adventuring, I am almost never in a position to escape entirely from business responsibilities. I may be able to take half a day for catfishing, but usually at least a half of every day has to be given over to intensive work.

As long as the Perry Mason television show is on the air, there are numerous responsibilities. Several times a week I have to dictate comments on television scripts, and there is a seemingly unending procession of mail and telegrams.

On this particular occasion when we started our trip of exploration, the television script department had gone on a part-time basis so some of the personnel could have a brief

Millie Conarroe can relax completely when there is nothing else to do.

summer vacation, and I anticipated fewer responsibilities for a couple of weeks.

Dick DeShazer, his wife, Moyne, Jean Bethell and Millie Conarroe were the other members of the party. Jean Bethell has been my chief executive secretary for many, many years and has accompanied me on nearly all of my travels as well as my exploring expeditions.

Millie Conarroe is an employer's dream of a secretary, thoroughly proficient in shorthand, typing, transcribing from dictating machines or typing directly from dictation. She is one of those rare individuals who doesn't get nervous when the heat is on, but simply settles down to the job and turns out more work than one would consider humanly possible; yet she can completely relax when there is nothing to do.

She had been one of my secretaries for many years, but when her husband was transferred to the northern part of the state I lost her. Since that time she had worked in various

50

law offices, and then, finding herself with a vacation on her hands, was only too glad to come back to the old job for some three weeks.

Later, we were joined by Anita Haskell Jones, a long-time friend who has been with me on many previous expeditions, and "Eddie" Walters, an expert yachtsman and friend of many years' standing, J. W. Black, his wife, Lois, and daughter, Jan.

We decided to use the River Queen as a secretarial office for the girls, as headquarters for the culinary department, as a place for general social gathering, and the Whit-Craft as a masculine dormitory where we men could retire from time to time while the secretaries were typing or cooking, and where we could do pretty much as we pleased.

It turned out to be an ideal arrangement.

I had intended to stretch the time of the first installment of our explorations into a long and variegated expedition, but

Lois Black and daughter, Jan.

The author and J. W. Black releasing a catfish.

once we found a beautiful place to tie up under towering shade trees on an uninhabited island with a little cove in which our smaller boats could nestle under wild blackberry bushes, I found myself becoming more and more a slave to the indescribable charm of living in a houseboat surrounded by every convenience that was worth a hang and free from all the annoying interruptions that do so much to build hypertension.

Our powerful radios could tune in just about any station we wanted. Our transistor-powered television set gave a small, brilliant image. We had walkie-talkies by which we could communicate readily over a distance of three or four miles, and, in case of emergencies, we had our radio telephones, which would put us in contact with civilization.

Every afternoon we would descend the swimming ladders in the back of the boats for a long, lazy period in the waters, which were just about the right temperature to be cooling

We tie up on an uninhabited island.

A long, lazy swim.

without being cold enough to curtail the time spent swimming or floating.

The radio brought us news of inland temperatures: 104 degrees at nearby Modesto, 121 degrees at some place in the South.

The Delta country, however, was cooled by breezes which funneled up through the Golden Gate. Starting at first near the river mouths as relatively strong winds, they dispersed into gentle, balmy, cooling breezes by the time they reached the island where we were anchored.

The nights were nearly always cool. I would go to sleep with a sheet blanket over me, then I would generally reach for an Army blanket before midnight, and then, sometime during the long restful period of sleep, would have roused myself enough for a second blanket before morning. However, my sleep-drugged reaction to the increasing coolness was automatic and left no memories which could be recalled in the morning. I would simply go to sleep under a sheet blanket and waken in the morning under two blankets— usually to hear the bubbling of the coffee percolator Dick had placed on the gas stove.

Having two separate houseboats tied up a few yards apart is a wonderful way to enjoy a vacation—the men on one, the women on the other—and while the women were constantly sweeping and tidying up their houseboat, we kept ours in a state of masculine informality which was a joy to behold.

I have always loved orderly disorder. That is, I am really a landlubber, and while the trained seaman has a place for everything and everything in its place, I have progressed to a point where I have a place for everything and everything someplace else.

I knew that I should be getting new material; I knew that I should be getting more photographs of different parts of the Delta country, but the charm of complete freedom from

The women were constantly tidying their boat. Jean Bethell and Moyne DeShazer.

care and responsibilities engulfed my consciousness in a state of utter tranquility. I was drugged with contentment.

Dick was, at first, inclined to be restless, and would start out in the morning in one of the smaller boats on trips of exploration, returning with fabulous stories of what he had found. I was, for the most part, willing to accept these stories and get the material secondhand. But when he discovered a little secret inlet where black bass were swarming around feeding so that the sucking sound was distinctly audible, I felt that it was time to take a camera, go out with him and see if we could get a photograph.

This time we took the fourteen-foot Valco, went down to this well-concealed cove, the surface covered by some type of vegetation which I was not enough of a botanist to recognize but which grew to the surface of the water, sent up leaves six or eight inches above the surface and then quit

55

growing. (I have since been told both that it is water hyacinth and water lilies.)

The bass were moving around in these patches of open water near the bank and occasionally making forays out into the floating weeds, apparently gathering some species of insect life which lived on the leaves or the upper part of the stems, because we could, from time to time, see their open mouths above the water and hear the gurgling noise made as they sucked in quantities of food-bearing water.

It proved to be virtually impossible to get photographs of a black bass on the dark surface of the shady water. However, it was completely fascinating to sit in the boat, keeping absolute silence, never moving so much as a muscle in a way which would cause the boat to transmit any sound and waiting for the bass to recover from the panic caused by our intrusion and get back to normal living.

We would sit there for minutes assuming, in patient impatience at first, what we felt would be comfortable positions but which would speedily develop into such cramped positions that it became necessary to move a foot an inch or two, to shift a hip to keep from sitting on the jackknife in a hip pocket or to swing around on the seat so that the sun was not reflecting right into the lens of the camera. It is surprising how many excuses a cramped posture can conjure up and how soon a body can become cramped.

The bass would come out and start working through the vegetation. First we would see the leaves moving; then we would get a glimpse of a ripple of water; then up would come the broad back of a bass, which would be visible for a moment and then vanish in moving vegetation, which was so thick that all we could see was the movement of the leaves.

Dick, who has the trained eye of a hunter, would point out many of these places where the bass were working. My eyes, which had spent far too many years scanning galley

Dick DeShazer waits with patient impatience.

proofs, television scripts and office work, had difficulty in getting the exact spot lined up.

Recognizing my inability to see what was so visible to him, Dick would move his forefinger eloquently in a series of silent, jabbing motions which said, in effect, "You damn land-lubber, can't you see that bass over there? Look! Take an-other look! *Right over there!*"

One bass was photographically co-operative. After minutes of swimming through the thick vegetation, he finally pushed his nose right up in front of the boat at a distance of about seven feet.

I felt certain that I could get a better photograph if I could only raise the camera angle, so I "noiselessly" elevated my creaking joints and cramped muscles to a semi-upright position.

57

Lee Ewoldt had a couple of good bass.

The result was a camera lens that was splashed with water. The bass gave one swift swirl, a flit with his tail and went downstairs so fast that he left only a vortex of swirling water behind him.

Eventually, however, after stalking a bass who was swimming around in the open for some twenty minutes, we located ourselves in a position of vantage in the leaves where Dick thought the bass might be coming on his next foray.

Sure enough, the fish started working toward us, and we had a period of several minutes of suspense while I was getting my camera ready, changing the distance on the focus scale from thirty to twenty, twenty to fifteen, fifteen to ten, and, finally, ten to six.

And then that bass, coming head-on, poked a great big snoot to within three feet of the boat. The light, however, was such that the dark water and the dark head of the bass blended together, so that I couldn't be sure of the picture.

I think that bass was completely preoccupied. As I took the picture, the boat swung around just enough so that a short oar which was trailing in the water rubbed against his head, and he was gone like a shot.

On a couple of subsequent occasions Dick and I ventured back into this sheltered cove, trying to duplicate our experience. We were never able to find the fish feeding the way we had found them on that first occasion.

I don't know whether it was the time of day, the state of the tide or whether there had perhaps been a hatch of flies which made the difference.

From time to time we would see the vegetation moving, showing that the bass were working deeper down in the water, and on rare occasions we would see one of the fish come up out of the water showing an expanse of back almost as big as the blade of an oar. But they didn't feed on the surface and continue feeding on the surface as they had that first time.

Primarily we were interested in getting photographs and not in getting fish. But with a proper lure it is apparently quite easy to catch these bass.

Early one morning Dick, Sam and I, in two boats, using paddles and oars, went gliding noiselessly around the point of the island and into this long inlet choked with vegetation.

We found a man sitting in a boat in our choice fishing spot, a man so thoroughly engrossed in what he was doing that he was apparently quite unaware of our approach.

This particular inlet was probably half a mile long and not over fifty yards wide. It was bordered by wild blackberry bushes and a tangle of vegetation. Here and there were open patches of water, but for the most part the surface of the inlet was simply a carpet of broad green leaves.

This fisherman turned out to be Lee Ewoldt, who has a rod and reel repair shop in North Sacramento, and there was no question but that he had been catching bass. He had been fishing for sport and turning back the bass that he didn't want to eat, but he had a couple of nice ones hanging on a string which he held up for us to see.

He was using a lure which was new to me. It had wire guards on it which prevented it from getting tangled in the dense vegetation, and he would cast it out, then bring it in, sliding through little openings or gliding over the leaves themselves to drop down in another little opening. The bass apparently were taking this rather readily.

He was a true fisherman, because he wanted to tell us about the big fish that had got away, the *"really* big fish" that had been on his line and then got loose. This had happened only a few moments before our arrival, and he was still excited about it.

All of which proves that fishermen are fishermen the world over.

It is always the big one that gets away.

On one of our trips in the mountains I was casting in a lake which had yielded only moderate-sized trout when I latched on to a really big one, a huge fish that fought my light tackle all over the lake.

Sam Hicks came along just as I was trying to land this fish. I had no landing net, and the fish was truly a monster.

"Sam," I yelled, "take off your shoes, get in there and see if you can ease up behind this fish so he doesn't break away when I try to get my fingers in his gill."

Sam obligingly took off his shoes. Later he had to take of his Levis as well. The shoreline was steeper than we had anticipated.

However, Sam got behind the exhausted fish and tossed it up on the bank.

I didn't take this fish directly into camp, but hid him in a snowbank about fifty yards away, then I walked on

Lee Ewoldt and bass.

in with my string of moderate-sized fish and let the others see I was all excited.

"Gee, you fellows had ought to see the monster that I latched on to there in the lake a few minutes ago," I said. "In all our fishing up here we haven't seen anything like that. Gee, he was a whopper! He was at least this long!"

The others promptly proceeded to take me down a notch. Every fish that got away was a whopper. How did I know he was a whopper? Fish would bite in a different way. Sometimes they would strike so that a relatively small fish felt like a monster, etc., etc.

Then they all laughed and said it was always the big ones that got away.

I looked at them in hurt surprise. "What do you mean, he got away?" I asked. "He didn't get away. I'm just storing him down in the snowbank to keep him cold."

Thereupon I walked back to the snowbank and returned

61

Moyne DeShazer and Jean Bethell gather wild blackberries from the housecruiser.

with this huge trout. I had the extreme pleasure of watching the expressions of incredulity on the faces of my companions.

Probably a word should be said about these wild blackberries in the Delta country. They grow in profusion along the banks, and with a boat it is possible to gather a big panful within a few minutes.

The house cruisers were ideal for blackberrying. They were high enough out of the water so that they got us into the choice upper tier of blackberries. They were strong enough so we could push them in on the banks without fear of consequences. We could stand at ease on the deck and take all the blackberries we wanted. And those wild blackberries, ripened on the vine to a state of perfection, made a wonderful breakfast dish.

From Striped Bass to Catfish

We ate blackberries with sugar and cream. We ate them with Corn Flakes, with Rice Chex. We ate them with toast. We ate them two and three times a day.

We would pick them from the vines, then put them in the refrigerator long enough to give them a good chill, then pour them into deep dishes.

We were probably too tenderhearted to fish because we weren't hungry enough and didn't need the fish.

However, our attitude toward catfish goes back to the time when I caught a beauty.

Now there is a trick to taking hold of a catfish. He has a long, wicked spine in his back fin and long, wicked spines in the two side fins. He also has a delightful trick of flapping his tail around so that his tail throws your hand against one of the sharp spines in the side fins.

But if you know how to handle a catfish and put the back

There is a trick to holding catfish.

I pushed his jaws open and he croaked his contempt.

spine between the first and second fingers of the left hand, get the thumb just underneath the lateral spike on the right side and the third finger just underneath the lateral spike on the left side, you can take the catfish off the hook without getting harpooned. Or you can hold him from the stomach side.

So I took hold of this catfish and tried to take the hook out of his mouth.

He wanted no part of me.

I have often thought of the courage of that catfish.

A moment before he had been swimming along the bottom of the slough in search of food. He had found what he thought was a choice morsel, had taken hold of it, felt a stabbing pain in his mouth and had abruptly been lifted out of his natural environment to confront a man who weighed a hundred and fifty times as much as he did.

The catfish knew this meant certain death.

But this catfish looked me in the eyes, clamped his jaws shut and refused to let me pry them open so I could get at the hook.

Finally I managed by main strength to push his jaws open.

He looked at me defiantly and uttered a deep guttural croak, showing his contempt.

That was the last straw.

I removed the hook from the mouth of the surprised catfish and tossed him overboard.

After that Sam and I decided we didn't need to eat catfish. We would get along without them. We took the barbs off our hooks and from time to time would catch catfish, putting them in a plastic tub, where we changed the water frequently, so that we kept them perfectly fresh. When we had a really good catch and were ready to go home, we photographed them, then dumped them all back into the water, so they could tell the other catfish about their experience—

We dumped them all back into the river.

doubtless being referred to as monumental liars by the other members of the community.

But it is fun to catch catfish. It is a lot of fun to sit in a comfortable folding chair on a shaded deck, letting your line hang down over the side, and feel the preliminary tug of an exploring catfish. Then the quick double tug which means he is really investigating and is a little mad that the bait doesn't come off easily. Then after about a second and a half comes the main tug, in which the fish says, "Well, I'll just show that bait it isn't so smart."

By timing a little twitch of the wrist at just the right moment, you can elevate Mr. Catfish up over the side.

And then after you have him in your hands it's a lot of fun to turn him loose.

The catfish, however, are smart. As soon as they feel the tug of a line, they make a lateral dash for the nearest snag and wrap the line around a sunken, waterlogged limb.

In some way they must realize there is a force at the other

66

end of that line that is bent upon their destruction, and instinctively they know the proper tactics to use to thwart that force.

Once Sam Hicks caught a catfish who had evidently bested an angler in this manner. The line had been wrapped around a snag and broken. The hapless catfish found himself imprisoned by his own strategy, snarled on a line wrapped around the dead limb of a submerged tree. The catfish had been forced to tear himself loose from the hook, leaving an ugly gap in his lower jaw.

One would have thought this catfish would never again have taken a bait, but appetites always overcome prudence and he had impaled himself on Sam's hook.

So we photographed him with his scarred lower jaw and threw him back to become a veritable Ananias among catfish, twice caught and twice freed, the greatest liar in the community.

This catfish had been caught before.

CHAPTER **4**

Marinas and Resorts

I knew that Dick was impatient to get the house cruisers into new territory. He wanted to take me on trips which would show me various aspects of the Delta country.

Ordinarily I am energetic to the point of being restless. I have never quite learned how to relax and do nothing. But the tranquil atmosphere of these house cruisers, the charm of sitting out on a shaded deck in a comfortable chair, watching the breeze rustle the leaves of the big shade trees, were utterly irresistible. I simply couldn't get up enough ambition or desire to go anywhere.

And I was enjoying the companionship, the feeling of being part of a friendly, cohesive group, isolated from the cares of the world.

There is one aspect of boating which is forcefully brought home to the observer as he becomes more familiar with it. There is a togetherness about all forms of boating which makes it a family pastime, particularly where there are children.

68

A friendly, cohesive group. Left to right: Jean Bethell, Moyne DeShazer, Millie Conarroe, Dick DeShazer and the author.

There is a togetherness about boating.

Boating brings out the whole family.

When we were exploring we would see camp after camp where headquarters was made on the yacht but where much of the family activity was on the sandy beach, where mother and father were swimming and enjoying themselves while the children were paddling around wearing life preservers or digging in the sand at the edge of the water.

Particularly on weekends the Delta country extends an invitation to families. Some of the groups would simply drive along the tops of the levees until they found a suitable picnic place. A light boat would be launched at the nearest ramp and then taken to the place where the family had gathered on a little strip of beach.

Sometimes groups would put up a canvas for shade, combining a couple of carloads of congenial families in one camp.

At other times families would rent houseboats for a vacation. While these rented houseboats average some forty-five dollars a day as the rental charge, it is to be remembered

70

they furnish sleeping and cooking quarters, swimming, sight-seeing and relaxation all in one package.

A family renting one of these boats for ten days at a cost of four hundred and fifty dollars has the means of a complete vacation, a rest for dad and mother, a paradise for the children, a healthful period in the outdoors, with interesting photographs, sunbathing, swimming, just plain resting and, when the vacation is over, something to talk about for many months.

A family of five or six could spend nearly this much simply stopping in motels and eating in restaurants without taking into consideration the myriad other expenses incident to steady travel. And, of course, in the sloughs there are a lot of houseboats both rented and privately owned.

I had had an opportunity to observe these family vacation groups on the way in to our secluded bay, where we tied the boats under big trees, whose trunks were nearly four feet in

Family parties dot the beaches.

Family group in The Meadows.

diameter. And, on a couple of occasions, when we went to Giusti's we saw quite a few of these yachting parties.

Giusti's (pronounced Jeoos-tees) needs a little explanation.

I have previously mentioned that all along the slough country there are little marinas and resorts, and these little resorts give an old-world charm to the Delta country.

For the most part they are operated by a husband and wife, a waitress and perhaps a dockhand. The places are small, the atmosphere is intimate and in some instances, when the woman is a talented cook, the place has far-reaching fame.

There is one restaurant which specializes in homemade pies, and people come from all over the Delta country to sit at the crowded counter and eat homemade pie, or to buy pies to take out on their boats.

Then there is the Beacon Resort, operated by Jim Muehlbauer and Troy Higgins. This place is noted in inland yachting circles for its breakfasts. Yachtsmen will travel long dis-

Some families arrive by car . . .

. . . and improvise shelter for the day.

Houseboats, both rented and privately owned . . .

. . . busily ply the sloughs on a fine day.

At Giusti's there is a warm friendliness and excellent food.

tances in order to sit down to the ham, bacon or sausage with eggs, fried potatoes and coffee which have made this establishment so famous.

In addition to the dining room, which looks out over the water, there is a large camping ground on a carpet of thick green grass. Many families spend their entire vacations here, alternately camping out in the shade, or fishing and cruising on their boats in the water.

Some miles farther up the channel Giusti's is operated by a family of Italian descent. The food is simply out of this world, a type of home cooking which brings back memories of really talented cooks whose greatest desire was to create dishes which were not only irresistible to the palate but satisfying to the inner man.

But the one thing about Giusti's which is distinctive is the atmosphere of warm hospitality which envelops the place.

Like all of these little levee resorts, Giusti's has a guest

75

Giusti's guest dock from the helicopter.

dock at which patrons can tie up their boats while they are patronizing the place, and there are, of course, gasoline pumps and facilities for filling the water tanks with good cool drinking water.

A long flight of wooden steps leads up from the water to the top of the levee, where a path stretches under the cool shade of a bearing fig trees across a road and on to a bar so dark and cool that at first one's sun-dazzled eyes have a hard time adjusting to the subdued light.

It is an orderly bar, a quiet little place, similar to that one would find if he were invited out to dinner and the host served drinks at a bar before dinner.

There are two key names to remember at Giusti's and they are both simple, Mo and Lo.

Mo stands for the head man, Manuel Morais, and Lo stands for the name of the bartender, Lorenzo Giannetti.

The buildings which house the bar and the dining room are

The author and "Mo" (Manuel Morias) at Giusti's dock.

long and narrow, although the dining room flares out into a little more width than the bar. This is partially because these buildings have one side perched at the edge of the road on top of the levee while the ground level is many feet below the buildings on the inland side.

In the fertile soil of the Delta country are gardens which grow crisp and tasty vegetables, and these vegetables in turn find their way into salads for Giusti's customers.

It is impossible adequately to describe the warmth of the place, the impression of hospitality, the cool crispness of the salads or the flavor of the food.

Many commercial resorts extend service on a basis of "Hello, Sucker! Come on in and be fleeced. We're as glad to have you as a kid is to entertain Santa Claus." But up at Giusti's there is warm friendliness, a genuine desire to accommodate. That atmosphere emanates from people who are happy with their lot in life and want you to be happy, too.

Giusti's has been in operation since time immemorial. The founder has long passed on; the present descendants are Irene Giusti and her daughter, Dolores. Mo married the daughter, and the whole family pitches in and runs the place.

The name Giusti's brings nostalgic memories to the minds of hundreds of yachtsmen who only hope that nothing will happen to change the atmosphere of the place or interfere with the wonderful cooking.

The little dining room will accommodate only a few people. The food is prepared with loving care, and the prices are those of yesterday.

Another interesting marina where we have spent considerable time, because I am keeping some of our boats stored there, is the one at Tiki Lagun, a place which is operated by Harold and Carol Taylor, some ten or fifteen miles west of Stockton.

This place is different from Giusti's in that while Giusti's

New docks being constructed at Tiki Lagun.

is old and rich in traditions of the old days and the old world, Tiki Lagun is rich in the enterprising spirit of American pioneering. It is an inspiration to see what the Taylors are accomplishing.

In many ways Tiki Lagun is pretty much of an operation bootstrap.

One gets the impression of old-world hospitality and enjoyment of life at Giusti's, while one gets the impression of indomitable will power, energy and determination at Tiki Lagun.

Harold Taylor and his wife, Carol, moved into Tiki Lagun without very much to go on less than two years ago. At that time the property had been used as a dump. It was littered with old tires, tin cans and tree roots. Taylor and his wife went to work — and how they worked! Simply because they were imbued with the spirit of American pioneering, they have built the place up, erected a long line of covered docks

Three weeks later the docks are almost finished.

and built a restaurant which serves home cooking and draft beer. These people are working as one seldom sees people work these days.

During the summer it is quite hot in the sun out in that part of the Delta country, and when one is building floating docks for boats and it becomes necessary to put on the roof, the carpenter working out in the open with the sun beating down from above and the roof reflecting the heat from beneath is being fried like a chicken on a spit.

But Harold and Carol have stayed with it, most of the time with only one helper, some of the time with no helper at all, putting up the docks, building up a business by steady, ceaseless toil. They are now just about over the hump, just reaching the point where they can settle back and take life a little easier.

But in the midst of all this atmosphere of hustle and bustle there is again that warm hospitality, that desire to give service.

I predict that this place will be one of the most successful marinas in the whole Delta country.

Carol runs the restaurant and, despite all the backbreaking work, finds time to bake some of her famous homemade cakes; and whenever anything goes wrong and any boat owner needs a helping hand, Harold is there as if by magic. Either Harold or Bill, his dockman, is always on the job.

The point is that the whole Delta country is dotted with these little places, each one having its own individuality, and it is a pleasure to move around and explore, searching out new places.

One can drift along the lagoons, tie up at the various guest floats, step from the glare into the cool, shaded seclusion of a bar, enjoy a cold drink and find as many different atmospheres as there are different places — and there are literally dozens of them scattered through the Delta country.

Tiki Lagun is rich in enterprising spirit.

CHAPTER 5

A Slight Problem with Power

When one is camping and has to carry water from a spring which may not be nearby, and cook everything which has to be cooked over a campfire which requires first the gathering of firewood and then letting it get down to coals, one is face to face with the essential verities of existence and takes little for granted.

The big trouble with house cruisers is that they so resemble expensive apartments that one comes to take too many things too much for granted.

When there are several women on a trip and dozens of electrical outlets and the various persons can plug in 110-volt electricity simply by flipping a switch, one tends to correlate the electricity with that furnished by high-power lines in the cities and may be prone to forget that this electricity is manufactured out in the wilds by a smoothly running generator. This generator operates so efficiently and quietly that one is inclined to forget that, after all, it is an independent machine operating on gasoline just like any other motor.

While we sometimes used charcoal, we relied a lot on electric percolators when we sat on the front deck, drinking coffee, and on the electric stove in the kitchen when we wanted something more substantial.

So that there is a second source of electricity, the River Queen is so designed that some of the lights and the water pump which puts pressure in the water tank operate from one of the storage batteries.

Now every one of us knew that the motor should be started every so often so that the batteries could be kept charged. The fact that we became so completely indolent and relaxed that we just kept taking everything for granted is probably one of the best endorsements of houseboat living one could conjure up.

From time to time we would try to remember just what day it was and just how long we had been living there in lazy luxury under the shade of those spreading trees. Invariably when we thought back on statistical dates, we expressed surprise that we had been there so long, but no one thought to translate time statistics into terms of gasoline consumed or batteries being run down.

Probably this was due to the fact that all these discussions would take place at night around the dinner table and there was always the nebulous "tomorrow" when we could "take care of all these matters."

Finally came the day when we decided it would be advisable to start the motors and charge the batteries.

These motors are equipped with electrical charging devices known as "alternators."

Now in all mechanical or electrical matters I am a complete moron. I can't tell the difference between the front end of a spark plug and the rear end of a differential. I take mechanical efficiency for granted and trust that my associates know what they are doing, because I know damn well that I don't.

Moyne DeShazer cooks by electricity in the open air and reads at the same time.

Therefore I dismissed all these mechanical details from my mind without even so much as a shrug of the shoulders. This was in the department of Sam and Dick.

Very much to our surprise when we threw the switch which was supposed to turn on the port motor on the River Queen, nothing happened.

A hurried investigation showed that the battery on the port side didn't have enough power to turn over the starter. Apparently everything on the port side had now gone dead.

Investigation as to the cause disclosed that some of the bedroom reading lights which operated on batteries had been considered by the feminine personnel to be simply part of the "system," and since the generator was working all right they had used whatever lights they wanted as long as they wanted. This had been going on for more than a week.

A Slight Problem with Power

Now this left us with a mechanical-electrical problem of major proportions. Everything on the port side of the boat was dead. We had a 110-volt generator which was working like a charm. We had the starboard engine and battery, which were in perfect working order.

Dick and Sam started a long, involved, expert discussion of how to get juice into the port battery so that it could start the motor, so that the motor could operate the alternator, which in turn could charge the battery.

As far as I was concerned, since it took the motor to start the engine which activated the alternator which charged the battery, and since the battery was too dead to start the motor so that the alternator could charge the battery, the problem was exceedingly simple. We were licked.

We were going to have to lift that dead battery out of the boat, take it in to Giusti's, pick up an automobile there, drive to Dick's place at Bethel Island and pick up another battery.

Charcoal is sometimes a necessity.

The World of Water

This is the simple, efficient type of reasoning which comes to a man who knows nothing of mechanical problems.

These experts on mechanical problems, however, had different ideas.

If we had had "jump wires," it seemed that we could have connected some battery "in parallel" and this would charge the dead battery enough to start the motor to operate the alternator to build up the charge in the motor.

Investigation showed we had no "jump wires."

Then the question arose whether we could take the current from the 110-volt generator and just touch the leads of the dead battery long enough to send in a current while we turned on the starter at exactly the same moment. Or whether we could disconnect the dead battery and in some way get the wires over to the battery on the generator.

All of this brought up the question of whether a discharged alternator would burn out if connected to a live battery, whether a 12-volt battery would recharge with a touch of 110-volt current, etc., etc., etc.

Dick DeShazer is an expert and, therefore, knows that a little knowledge is a dangerous thing. He was inclined to debate the matter and consider it thoughtfully.

Sam Hicks is a man of action.

Sam grabbed a screwdriver and started back to do something with the alternator.

I pleaded with him to stop.

I wanted time to debate the matter. I pointed out the possibility that while he was trying to fix the port engine he would put the 110-volt generator on the blink.

Trying to talk Sam into taking things easy during an emergency is like trying to stand on the stern of a boat and ask the tide not to come in.

Sam went into action. His theory was correct. He knew it was correct.

When we sit around on deck, the electric coffeemaker perks a great deal of the time.

I wailed long and loud, and to no avail.

Sam apparently had decided to take the wires from the 110-volt generator, shoot them momentarily into the dead 12-volt battery with the idea that electricity would somehow create electricity just as people make people.

In the meantime we had dinner cooking in the electric kitchen, which was powered by the 110-volt electric generator. This generator, apparently terrified at Sam's technique with the screwdriver, promptly proceeded to give up the ghost as soon as Sam touched the wires.

Dinner was half cooked when the stove went from red-hot to lukewarm, from lukewarm to cold.

Now we had a dead port engine, a dead port battery and a dead 110-volt generator.

As I have remarked, this house cruiser is equipped with all the refinements of a high-class apartment.

The trouble was we had put them all on the fritz.

Whit-Craft slung in carrier.

We had an air conditioner which wouldn't work, a port engine which was dead, an alternator which wouldn't work, a 110-volt generator which had lost its polarity — according to the experts (I don't know what polarity is) — a stove which was cold, water tanks filled with water which we couldn't pump out through the faucets, bedroom lights which were supposed to turn on soft reading lights. None of the gadgets would work. We had everything arranged for an appetizing dinner, but the dinner was rapidly turning cold after being half cooked. Deep dusk was closing in and we had no lights to turn on.

Since we were so abundantly equipped with all the conveniences, it had never occurred to anyone to bring a bundle of good old-fashioned candles.

So it became readily apparent that everybody was going to have to move over to the Whit-Craft, finish cooking the dinner on our butane gas stove over there and turn on lights from our generator, which, in turn, was powered by a motor equipped with an alternator and in which there hadn't been any reversal of polarity.

The idea of having our masculine dormitory invaded by a group of determined women, equipped with cooking utensils, dishrags, dish towels, brooms, mops and references to masculine untidiness, was singularly uninviting.

Going without dinner was also uninviting.

Now Dick has one young man working for him who is fully familiar with all the electrical gadgets in connection with these houseboats. I suggested that we try to locate this man by telephone.

It was long after closing hours and Dick wasn't certain whether he could get him, or where we could get him, but we decided to use our ship-to-shore radio telephone and see what could be done. However, it was certain the guy couldn't get there in time to do any good as far as the immediate emergency was concerned.

Process of lifting Whit-Craft from the water.

Dick DeShazer, Richard Whittaker, and the author holding a powwow.

I did derive some pleasure from the situation because I was able to point out to all and sundry that I had begged and pleaded with Sam not to monkey with the generator wires in order to try to revive the dead port engine.

This gave no one else any satisfaction whatever, but it gave me such a high degree of pleasure that I really felt I could get through a dinnerless evening without dying before morning. I was a martyr and I wanted everyone to know it. Whenever Sam looked at me, which he did as infrequently as possible, I let him know that I was a martyr by the woebegone expression of extreme resignation on my face. Occasionally I would take a deep breath and force a wan smile so everyone would know I was being a good sport about it and wasn't really holding it against Sam — after all, the guy had tried — even if he hadn't listened.

Then at a time when our spirits had reached an all-time low and we were trying to find out how we might get in

A group of young people rendezvous for a day of water skiing.

Clam digger at work for bait.

touch with Dick's mechanic, Dick perked up his ears and said, "Was that a cry for help?"

We listened, and sure enough here came another high-pitched call.

We dashed out of the interior of the houseboat prepared to throw out life preservers and what have you, and then paused in amazement.

On the opposite bank of the slough at a place where a person could park an automobile and then, by walking three or four hundred yards, reach the bank, stood Dick's young mechanic, plainly visible in the twilight.

But the mechanic was resplendent in a spotless white nylon sweater, carefully creased blue slacks and, as it subsequently turned out, carefully shined shoes.

With a glad cry of welcome, we sent the Valco skimming over the water to the other side of the slough, picked up the mechanic and brought him aboard.

He said he had made the trip to bring some important letters for Dick, but his eyes kept roving to Millie.

Millie is about his age. She is very easy on the eyes, and since she and her husband were divorced after she left my employ, it became painfully obvious that the mechanic had not arrived to fix motors, that his call was intended to be social.

To hell with that stuff!

We had that white sweater off the guy in seconds. We crowded him down in the hold with the reverse polarity, the dead alternator, the lifeless battery, the generator which wouldn't generate and all the rest of it.

Sam was trying to explain what he had done. I was talking at the same time, telling the mechanic for heaven's sake not to listen to Sam or they would louse up the starboard motor on the boat, which, at the moment, was the only thing that was running.

Millie Conarroe is easy on the eyes.

Millie stood by demurely, looking very attractive, but showing by her expression that she assumed, *of course,* the guy had come up simply to fix the engines and deliver mail to Dick.

When Sam Hicks gets an idea in his head, it lodges between his ears, and I have never found any way of getting it unlodged. One could put a charge of T.N.T. in Sam's left ear, an atomic bomb in his right ear and detonate both of them simultaneously. The skull would disintegrate and disappear, but the idea would still be there, intact and in its original form.

So Sam kept insisting that his treatment of whatever it was he had done was theoretically one that should have produced results.

In the meantime my acid comments reached a new height

93

of sarcasm and I was all but on my knees begging somebody to try to get that damn screwdriver out of Sam's hand and keep him from descending on the one good starboard motor.

It was at this point that a brilliant idea struck Sam. He got a measuring stick and tested the gasoline in the tank that ran the 110-volt generator.

This was one of those coincidences which can happen only once in a million years, nevertheless, it *had* happened on our boat that night. The generator had run out of gasoline at the exact moment Sam descended on it with a screwdriver, trying to reverse the polarity of the alternator or whatever the hell it was he was doing.

So they took gasoline from one of the other tanks, put it in the gasoline tank which fed the 110-volt generator, the generator promptly started generating and then Sam carried out the rest of his wild-eyed scheme and the port motor started running. Dick called back directions about tapping something or other to bring the points of the regulator into proper position. The ammeter showed a steady charge pouring into the battery, from the revived alternator the lights came on, the stove warmed up and everything ran smoothly.

I took myself over to the Whit-Craft and stretched out on my bunk to recuperate.

Sam was very nice; he didn't say anything.

When I got back into circulation, the lights were blazing on the River Queen, the dinner was piping-hot and ready to be served. The mechanic's glistening white sweater had been retrieved, and the mechanic and Millie had gone out to dinner.

Truly, a good secretary is a gift of the gods.

CHAPTER **6**

The Beauty of The Meadows

As I have previously mentioned, there are various types of boats designed for various uses. These uses are many and diverse.

Water skiing is rapidly growing in popularity. I am too "mature" to become a water skier, but I can appreciate the joy of the sport.

The boat most desired by the water skier is a light, fast boat with a powerful motor, which will send it skimming at high speed over the surface of the water and at the same time furnish enough extra power to tow one or two skiers behind.

The wake of such a boat makes waves. Water skiing also makes waves.

Waves can be inconvenient to a moored boat and at times downright destructive.

A steady procession of waves tearing away at the bank of a levee can do a considerable amount of damage.

Water skiing is rapidly growing in popularity.

Therefore for the most part the water skiers get or try to get into places where they will not disturb others with their wakes and where the waves will do little or no damage to the structure of the levees.

This isn't always the case, however, because there are just too many water skiers. Some are ignorant, some discourteous, but for the most part the good water skier is a sportsman who is careful to select a place where his wake will cause a minimum of damage.

The good water skier is apt to be a superb physical specimen, whether male or female, and is a joy to behold. However, some of the best of them come to grief at times and get dunked.

To the north of Giusti's there is one wide, beautiful lagoon which has, by a species of gentleman's agreement, been declared off limits to water skiers. It is tacitly understood that this is where family parties with children go for their camp-

A light fast boat is necessary for water skiing.

Water skiing makes waves disturbing to houseboaters.

Water skiers try to find secluded places.

Ken Brown of Mountain View, California, an excellent water skier.

A skier in the drink.

ing, where cruisers can drop anchor and tie up with a stern line without being subjected to continual rocking from wakes of high-speed boats.

In fact, there is a general rule in the Delta country, which is, I believe, backed up by a county ordinance, to the effect that a man is responsible for his wake, and in places where other boats are moored, or in the vicinity of any marinas, the speed limit is five miles an hour. This is specifically to prevent damage from the wakes of passing boats.

The lagoon which has been set aside for cruisers, houseboats, etc., and where water skiing is taboo, is known as "The Meadows," and it is one of the most beautiful areas of inland waterway I have ever seen.

To reach The Meadows one has to go under a bridge, after negotiating a narrow channel.

The shoreline on both sides is covered with a heavy growth of trees, and it is possible to drop a bow anchor, put the

99

To reach The Meadows, one goes under a bridge.

cruiser in reverse, put out a stern line which is tied to a tree and have a secure mooring, fore and aft.

The result is that The Meadows has a whole series of cruisers tied up side by side along with houseboats, some of which are privately owned, some of which are rented, some of which are amphibian; using wheels, they double as house trailers on land.

Some of the cruisers are large and expensive. Some are small and relatively inexpensive, but the owners are motorboat enthusiasts who love the water and love boats.

Not only do they have this love of boats in common but boat owners who make it a habit to come to The Meadows get to know one another and a social life develops along with a spirit of camaraderie.

Sometimes one will encounter a group of several cruisers not only anchored abreast but tied together.

In this part of the Delta the Army Engineers have not as

Negotiating a narrow channel.

Cruisers in The Meadows.

An amphibious houseboat. Wheels enable it to become a housetrailer
on land.

yet enforced their shade-destructive edict that all trees must
be removed from the banks.

Apparently the levees do become safer and stronger when
all vegetation is removed and the denuded slopes are faced
with rocks. At least this is the present theory of the Army
Engineers. (If this theory should prove to be fallacious, it is
going to be tragic because it would take years to replace the
shade trees which are being torn out.)

Even if this theory is correct, it would seem that the new
dams which have been or are being erected will control the
floods in the rainy season to such a point that the trees can
remain on the levees.

These shaded levees furnished picnic and fishing spots for
many families looking for a chance to get out on a Sunday
afternoon for recreation.

Now miles and miles of trees have been torn out. The once

Levees denuded of shade trees . . .

. . . and reinforced with rock.

Skier on a short rope.

A shady berth for cruisers.

We find a stranger (Lee Ewoldt) in our "secret" spot for bass fishing.

picturesque lagoons and sloughs have become mere canals fenced in by rock-faced levees. California has lost much of its scenic and recreational charm as a result.

If within the next three or four years we are told that our system of dams has lessened the damages of floods, the barren, treeless levees with the rock face reflecting shimmering heat will be a tragic reminder of our national disregard for natural beauty, our passion to destroy and change in blind worship of the god of efficiency.

At least we can hope The Meadows escapes this orgy of destruction and that conditions which have existed for a hundred years in safety won't be destroyed in the name of efficiency.

CHAPTER **7**

A Yachtsman in Distress

There is one inviolable rule of yachting which should be noted parenthetically. It is that any yachtsman will at any time go to the help of a brother yachtsman in distress.

We had made our headquarters in the north end of Snodgrass Slough, which is open to water skiers and a few miles to the north of The Meadows. For the most part, skiers kept pretty much to the center of the channel as they went by, so they didn't give our boats too great a rocking, but occasionally someone would cut across the stern of one of the boats and really give us a bad time.

Therefore I thought it might be a good plan to take a look at The Meadows and see if we wanted to move headquarters up there.

So Sam and I got in the Valco, took some cameras and went skimming along Snodgrass Slough under the bridge

106

and up into The Meadows to look at the cruisers anchored there.

Here, of course, we slowed down to a pace that was hardly more than a walk, and I took a few pictures of some of the more luxurious boats that were anchored up there.

We went to the end of the slough and turned to start back.

As I have said before, I am a landlubber, but given a yachting cap with a little gold braid on it, I can look very nautical and convincing.

So when we started back and one of the cruisers began to frantically blow its horn and the owner came out and waved his cap at us, Sam assumed it was someone we knew.

I, however, had a horrible premonition.

"If that man wants help," I told Sam, "he's come to just about the worst place in the world to get it."

Sam, who had his screwdriver in the toolbox, said nothing.

The horn continued to toot and the man continued to make motion.

"We can't disregard a summons like that," Sam said, and turned the boat in toward the cruiser.

My worst suspicions were confirmed. "Can you help me?" the man asked.

"No," I said.

Sam's face lit up. He reached for his screwdriver. "What seems to be the trouble?" he asked.

"I got my boat in here, tied it up and now I can't get it started again."

Fresh from his triumph with reversing the polarity of our alternator, beating the points of our regulator into submission and giving a quick shot of life to a dead battery so that it would start, Sam was literally overflowing with self-confidence.

I felt I simply *had* to prevent him getting aboard that cruiser at all costs.

107

The World of Water

"We can take you to a telephone," I suggested. "We can take you over to the other bank on the mainland. It's only a short walk to Walnut Grove. You can get help there."

"I'd like to get the motor started," the yachtsman said.

I could see Sam starting to drool.

"Perhaps the next boat down the line has a ship-to-shore telephone," I suggested.

"Well," the yachtsman said, "we might try that."

Sam tried to conceal his disappointment as the yachtsman climbed aboard.

We went to the adjoining cruiser.

"Do you have a ship-to-shore telephone?" the yachtsman asked.

His neighbor nodded.

"Can you summon help?"

"Sure thing. What's the trouble?"

The yachtsman told him.

"Come aboard," the neighbor invited, picked up the telephone, turned it on to the Coast Guard channel and said, "Coast Guard, come in, please. Over."

Three minutes later the trouble had been explained. The Coast Guard had told us to stand by while it notified a Coast Guard Auxiliary Patrol, then called back and said, "Within ten minutes help will arrive."

So we went out in the channel to meet the help as it arrived, and it wasn't over five minutes before that Coast Guard Auxiliary Cruiser came gliding along.

Of course, Sam and I and the small boat were commissioned to get the dinghy from the rescuing cruiser put behind the disabled cruiser, get the towline transferred from one boat to the other and stand by until the tow got under way.

All this was a rather time-consuming task, but even so, it beat having Sam get aboard that unsuspecting owner's yacht and start work with his screwdriver.

Sam and I went up to The Meadows to look at the cruisers anchored there.

Now I am perfectly willing to admit that Sam's hunch was right on our own boat, but I would have hesitated to see him reversing the polarity (or whatever the heck it is he does with his screwdriver) on the boat of a total stranger.

But as we saw the disabled boat being towed slowly down through the channel and started for home, I realized that our troubles weren't over.

The neighboring cruiser gave us a hail. He was, it seems, having trouble getting his anchor to hold. Would we mind picking up his bow anchor, taking it out to the limit of the

109

The Sheriff's Patrol saves a boat from sinking . . .

rope, dropping it overboard gently and seeing if we could find a holding ground for the cruiser?

"Not at all."

We picked up the dripping anchor, held it alongside the little Valco, went out to the limit of the rope and dropped the anchor into the water.

Then we stood by while the yachtsman waited for the anchor to settle and get a good hold. He put tension on the line, then waved his thanks and good-bye.

I looked at my watch.

I knew that the folks back in the house cruisers would be worried about us. We were long overdue.

"Sam," I said, indicating the dozens of yachts between us and the main channel, "let's get out of here fast. Appearances are deceptive. We look too nautical."

"We're not suppose to leave any wake in these waters," Sam pointed out.

110

. . . by pushing it into shallow water.

"Rev the motor up and this boat will get on the surface of the water and won't leave a ripple," I told him.

I kept my eyes focused straight ahead so that we wouldn't see any more distress signals, feeling that we had done our good turns for the day, and we got out of there.

But one has to marvel at the efficiency of the Coast Guard. It gives one a feeling of security. Sometimes a man can feel proud of being a taxpayer.

There is also the Sheriff's Patrol. I don't know how many boats the sheriffs have in the Delta country, but we see them every so often on patrol, and Sam ran on one of them making a rescue. A cruiser had somehow sprung a big leak, and water was coming in faster than the occupants could bail it out.

One of the Sheriff's Patrol boats put in a prompt appearance, tied on to the sinking boat and supported it long enough to get it beached where it could be repaired.

Just as the speedboats and water skiers tend to congregate

111

The sailboats gather in Lost Slough.

These sailboats are expertly handled.

It is interesting to watch these men manipulate their boats.

in certain districts in the Delta, so the sailboats tend to gather in Lost Slough.

I don't know whether this is because it is difficult for them to go any farther because of tall masts and a drawbridge which crosses the main slough and which opens only at fixed intervals, or whether there is something about the waters in Lost Slough which appeal to the sailing enthusiasts.

Whatever the reason, one will be almost certain to find a group of sailboats clustered at the head of Lost Slough. These vary from big tall-masted yachts to the little one-man boats with small triangular sails.

It is interesting to watch these men manipulate their boats, guiding them solely by wind power, yet turning and twisting them in the channel with the greatest of ease. One would think these boats were powered by some invisible propellant — as indeed they are. But using the wind as motive power is tricky and calls for skill of a high order.

113

CHAPTER 8

Restaurants Along the Levee

Not only are there some marvelous eating places scattered along the banks of the levees in these little family resorts, but some of the best restaurants in the world are in the Delta country.

Here again, many of them would impress the newcomer as being little hole-in-the-wall places, but actually, beneath the somewhat drab exteriors, they serve excellent food.

Just across the bridge going to Bethel Island is a little restaurant known as "Wanda's," which, when I first knew it, was operated by a young woman who managed to serve the guests, take the orders, do the cooking, and presumably the dishwashing as well.

Now the place has expanded, but there is still a delightful atmosphere of home cooking about it. A little farther down the street and on the other side is Irving Podre's "Bel-Isle Club," a place which features both Chinese and American cooking and has a bar which sells packaged goods as well as liquor by the drink.

The place is exceedingly popular, and during the rush hours on Friday, Saturday and Sunday nights it is all but impossible to get a parking place anywhere near it.

It has cooks who really understand their business, and its Chinese combination dinners are "out of this world"!

For those who want American food, it specializes in a "rib eye steak," which is about as delicious a piece of meat as one can ever hope to find.

Here again, there is a friendly, informal atmosphere about the place. People come in just as they are and are made welcome.

When one sees the number of people waiting to be served, one naturally wonders why these places don't expand; but once they begin to expand, they have labor troubles and all the other problems incidental to growing pains. Most of the places seem to prefer to keep their individuality and remain small.

One of the exceptions to the rule is the "River View Lodge" restaurant at Antioch, where one can dine looking out over the water.

No matter how this place might expand, however, it would still have a waiting line during the weekend rush hours. The food is, for the most part, seafood but usually there are steaks, too, and about the best extra-cut prime ribs of beef I have ever tasted.

This place also specializes in cheese bread. I don't know exactly how it is prepared but, presumably, the chef takes very, very fresh sourdough French bread, cuts it in slices, covers it with butter and puts on a sauce made of blended cheeses. Then the whole thing is placed in a hot oven and the cheese and butter melt and soak through the bread.

I have noticed that one of the outstanding features of many of these restaurants in the Bay Area is the very, very fresh sourdough French bread.

Water skiing looks easy from a helicopter.

To me, there is nothing quite so appetizing and satisfying as a cut of really fresh sourdough French bread with a glass of red wine. I could make a meal of it if I had enough French bread, enough butter and enough wine. I doubt if I could ever get enough.

Evidently some of these restaurants get shipments of bread while the loaf is right fresh out of the oven. I presume they must have several bread shipments a day — but the sourdough French bread is as fresh as the oven can make it.

There is also a Mexican restaurant at Brentwood, which serves *real* Mexican food and has genuine, imported Mexican beer to go with it.

The prices are absurdly low, and apparently the restaurant doesn't care about tourist trade. A person could drive by the

116

place a dozen times and have no idea that a restaurant was there. However, the old-time residents of the Delta know of the place and make it a rule to go there from time to time.

It is not necessary to speak Spanish, but it will help if you do. You will find the restaurant pretty well filled with persons of Mexican descent, and there is a jukebox which has a large selection of records in Spanish.

The food, the real Mexican McCoy, is individually cooked to order and served bubbling-hot.

There are other very famous restaurants in Antioch — places where, I am told, food will literally melt in your mouth — but having to watch my weight and being inclined to go back to the places I like, I simply haven't as yet got around to them.

Expert skiing.

CHAPTER **9**

Ghost Towns of the Delta

Part of the charm of the Delta country lies in the general atmosphere which envelops the place.

Sacramento has grown by leaps and bounds and is a big city.

Greater San Francisco, at the other end of the road, is, of course, a teeming metropolis.

Yet between these urban areas lies a stretch of country which in places is virtually unchanged from what it was many decades ago.

There are several reasons for this. One of them is the peculiar physical nature of the terrain.

The soil is for the most part a peat soil, and peat soil is peculiar in that it will float, it will burn and it will blow away in a really strong wind. In fact, wind erosion is one of the problems these ranchers have to contend with.

On the other hand, peat soil is tremendously fertile and productive. Over ninety percent of the white asparagus crop in the world is grown in the peat soil of the Delta region.

118

The level of the farms may be twelve or fifteen feet, or perhaps more, below the water line. Therefore the water is contained in sloughs, canals and channels by high levees.

At the time these levees were built, no one realized the tremendous potential value of waterfront property.

There are places on the sloughs along Bethel Island and some of the other sloughs where this waterfront property has been reclaimed, so to speak, and beautiful residences are built at least in part on the levee so that there is a view of the water from picture windows in the living room and there are also private docks down on the water.

For the most part, however, in those earlier days when highways were being planned, the tops of the levees seemed the logical location.

So throughout the whole Delta district the tops of the levees are very likely to have roads, while the ground some twenty feet below is planted to crops.

The fields on the left are below water level.

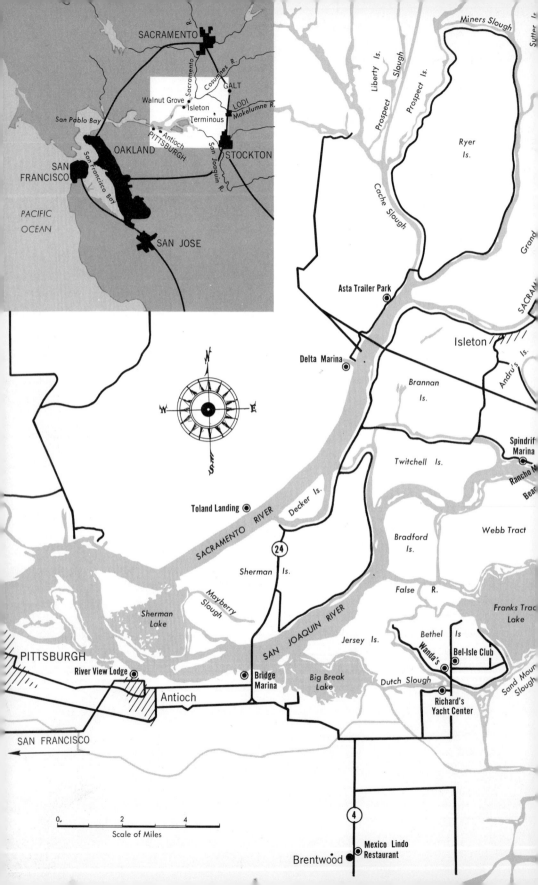

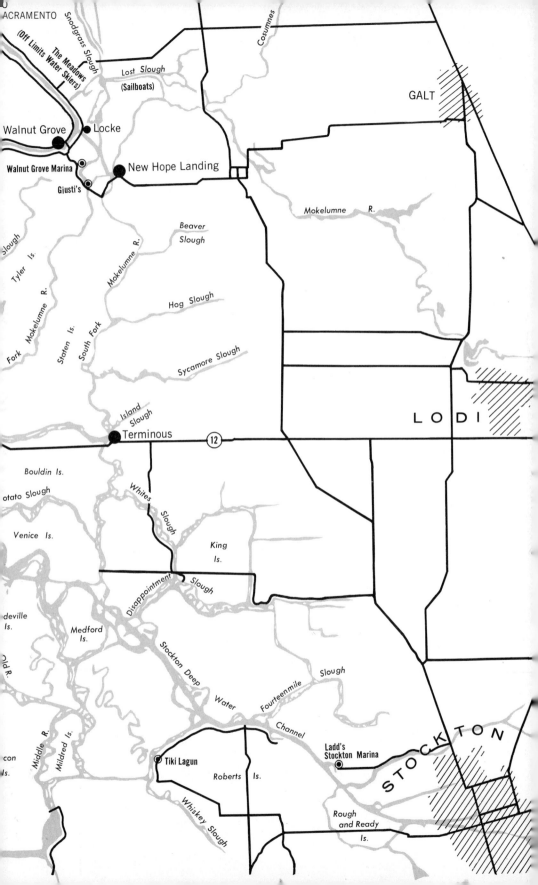

The World of Water

This farming land is very rich, and the persons who hold it just don't seem to be interested in making a sale. Therefore the whole territory tends to remain very much as it has been for years and years.

There are many auto ferries in the Delta, ferries which take vehicles for perhaps no more than a long city block across channels from one island to another. These ferries are pulled over and back on cables which sink to the bottom when not being used.

The ferries haul school buses, farm workers, produce trucks and autos.

On the other hand, many children are taken back and forth to school in boats and much of the mail is delivered in boats, the post office boxes being located at the ends of short piers.

Those wider roads which are not constructed on the levees

The railroad drawbridge is open all the time, except when a train is coming. Then it automatically closes until the train has passed. Note the roads on top of the levees.

Island Ferry.

River Ferry.

Post boxes are on the water. This one serves Mandeville Island.

but on the lower land have a terrific drainage problem. The water table may be, and usually is, quite close to the surface in many parts of the Delta region.

All of these factors have tended to hold back the development of subdivisions, superhighways, etc., and the Delta country remains something of an isolated island in an encroaching sea of civilization which at times threatens to engulf all the old landmarks in the adjoining country.

Scattered along the main river channels are little towns which fifty years ago were supplied mainly by riverboats.

These big river freighters have now been retired from service, and the West has suffered a great loss as a result.

It seems incredible that these huge boats, with their shallow draft, could have navigated the Sacramento River through fog and darkness, arriving unerringly at their destination; but they were built for the job and they were piloted by men

The *Navajoa*, one of the big river boats, is now located in a peat field.

The *Navajoa*.

A palatial river boat, the *Delta King*, moored just below Stockton . . .

. . . and a close-up of the *Navajoa*.

who were experts. They made the trip winter and summer, night after night.

One of these boats, the *Navajoa,* is now located in the middle of an island peat field. There are various stories as to how it got there.

One story is that during a period when the levee had broken the big boat was piloted in through the break so that its powerful engines could be used to pump out the water as the levee was being repaired.

Another story is that the owners of the ranch, looking for a place to house the farm labor imported from Mexico, found they could purchase the boat cheaper than they could erect any type of living quarters.

Perhaps both stories are correct.

Another of these palatial riverboats, *The Delta King,* is moored just below Stockton.

These boats were huge affairs, with several decks above the freight deck, and they represented the last word in luxury. The new superhighways, new bridges and higher speed limits put them out of business.

Many years ago when the highway between San Francisco and Sacramento was narrow and tortuous, before the days of the Golden Gate and the Carquinez Strait bridges, traveling from San Francisco to Sacramento by automobile was something of a nightmare, involving trips on two automobile ferries with all the incident delays.

In those days the riverboats did a thriving business. One could drive his automobile onto the boat in San Francisco, rent a luxurious stateroom and enter a dining salon where meals must have been served virtually at cost because the line prided itself on its low prices.

After dinner one could stroll on the deck, then settle down to a night's sleep in his cabin, listening to the swish . . . swish . . . swish . . . of the big paddle wheel of the boat, watch the banks of the river go gliding by, seemingly within only a few feet of the boat rail, waken in the morning tied up in Sacramento, drive his car off and start the trip from Sacramento fresh as the proverbial daisy.

I used to make this trip often on business, and there were many others who made it for pleasure, particularly on weekends.

Some of these boats are now rather dilapidated, but here and there one can find a trace of the pride of bygone days: a carved ornamental stair rail or bits of Oriental teak which have survived the elements.

The riverbank cities which were supplied by these boats have for the most part remained pretty much as they were in the days of river traffic.

The city of Locke in particular is unique, although the nearby town of Walnut Grove has taken on much of the flavor of Locke.

There are conflicting stories as to how Locke got started and what went on there, and there are even conflicting stories as to what is there now.

One story is that during the period when Orientals were forbidden by California law to hold real estate, the owners of the huge ranch at Locke permitted the Chinese to come in and put up buildings.

Regardless of what the true explanation may be, the fact remains that Locke is almost entirely Chinese and retains the Oriental atmosphere. Chinese sit on hard benches, resting and gossiping.

There was a time when the town was practically "wide open." Now it gives the outward appearance of a ghost city. But if one prowls around, one can find here and there interesting bits of local color which are thoroughly tantalizing.

There is, for instance, a side street market operated by Chinese in so secluded a place that you virtually have to know

Our two house cruisers stop for gas.

Delta country from the air.

The setting sun gilds a pathway.

A pair of accomplished water skiers.

Auto ferry crossing Tiki Lagun.

Where the big bass feed.

A perfect solution to a warm day.

Jean Bethel and Sam Hicks in the Smithcraft.

Some of the old river boats have become headquarters for yacht clubs and restaurants.

that the side street and the market are there in order to find the place.

Yet it is a relatively big market, and it not only has exotic Chinese foods which I have long craved but have been unable to buy elsewhere but it also has all the modern groceries and some of the best meat one can buy.

For many years when I was practicing law I represented Chinese clients. Those were the days when the city of Oxnard, where I had hung out my shingle, had a large, well-organized Chinatown.

At the start I represented a few of these clients in misdemeanor cases involving Chinese lottery and fan-tan, and because I enjoyed a spectacular success in these early cases I soon found myself the official attorney of Chinatown.

At first the Chinese had a lawyer from Los Angeles on the big cases. He was known as *Tai Chong Tze,* or The Big

129

The World of Water

Lawyer; while as the local lawyer I was known as *Chong Tze T'oy,* or The Little Lawyer.

Came the case when I had the brilliant inspiration of confusing the detectives (stool pigeons in the vernacular) by a scheme worthy of my fictional character, Perry Mason.

The police had made some twenty-one arrests, and I had a shrewd suspicion that the imported detectives couldn't tell one Chinese from another, but were making identifications purely from notes they had taken on the places of residence of the various defendants.

So I shuffled Chinatown. I put Lip Kee over in Chew Boc Chung's place of business. I put Chew Boc Chung over at Lim Lung's store, and so on, down the line.

The district attorney decided his strongest case was against one Wong Duck, and so they went to Wong Duck's place of business to drag Wong Duck over to jail to await trial. (The Chinese were all out on bail, which was increased when they were taken in for trial, so that the police would in effect come and rearrest the Chinese the district attorney wanted.) The idea of this was that the Chinese might feel it was better to "jump bail" than to stand trial and pay a lawyer's fee.

It was just as the police were taking the Chinese who was in Wong Duck's place of business into custody to be transported over to the county seat that one of the sheriff's deputies, who had the knack of recognizing Orientals and being able to tell one from another, said, "Wait a minute, boys, this isn't Wong Duck!"

The detectives swore up and down that this *was* the Wong Duck who had sold them a Chinese lottery ticket. They swore they could recognize him.

(There was some truth in this because the man posing as Wong Duck had indeed sold them a ticket, but at an entirely different place of business.)

An argument developed. The man insisted he wasn't Wong

130

Chinese sit on benches, gossiping. The author, far right, practices on his long-unused Cantonese.

Duck. The deputy sheriff didn't think he was Wong Duck. But he had been apprehended at Wong Duck's place of business and the detectives swore by all that was holy that the man was Wong Duck.

That night the Oxnard paper carried a big headline: WONG DUCK MAY BE WRONG DUCK SAYS DEPUTY SHERIFF.

The harassed district attorney threw in the sponge and quit on all the cases.

The grateful Chinese got their bail money back, each returned to his own place of business and thereafter I became *Tai Chong Tze*, The Big Lawyer.

I have always been interested in Orientals, and particularly the Chinese. From time to time I picked up a little Cantonese, and then came the time when I went to China and spent some time prowling around, getting local color for a series of

The World of Water

Chinese stories, going from Macao in the south to Peking in the north.

It has been thirty-odd years since I have talked Chinese to any extent, but I still remember enough of it to get by. So when I walked into this market at Locke and sensed that they didn't particularly care for outside customers, I started throwing a little Chinese around and in a short time had sparked a friendly contact.

There are some delightful things about the Chinese language.

For one thing, Cantonese is a language of monosyllables and since each monosyllable has to represent more than one word meaning, the inflection, or tone, distinguishes what meaning the word has. There are also words of almost the same sound.

For instance, *gow* is dog, and *ngow* is cow.

All in all, there are eight main tones in the Cantonese language, which accounts for the fact that when an Occidental tunes in on a Cantonese conversation the Chinese seem to be talking in a singsong.

Few people know that each subtle tone change means a change in the meaning of the word.

Because this is true, it is impossible to use a rising inflection to indicate a question in Cantonese. Therefore the Chinese question mark is oral and consists of the word *mah* at the end of a sentence.

When two Chinese greet each other, one is apt to say to the other, *"Hoh shai kai mah,"* which, translated, means "Is the whole world good?"

The man to whom the inquiry is addressed will bow his head and say, *"Hoh shai kai,"* which means, "The whole world is good."

On the other hand, if you ask a Chinese merchant if he is enjoying good business, *"Nay yeu hoh sahng yee mah,"* he will almost never agree with you, but reply, *"M'hoh, m'hoh, sahng yee. Sahng yee m'hi gay hoh. Hoh dahm,"* meaning, "Business is not much good; things are very quiet now."

Chinese have an inherent fear of admitting the possession of wealth or good business. In China the merchant who is unduly prosperous can expect to be kidnapped, robbed or, if he takes a trip on a boat, beset by pirates. Therefore the wealthy always try to conceal their wealth.

Palatial residences will have a wall running around them, and on the street side of the wall will be numerous little shack houses, occupied by people who are quite evidently far from affluent. The owner of the palatial mansion will have a secret entrance through one of these little shacks, and hopes thereby to fool the lawless into thinking he is a poor mark for any depredation or kidnapping for ransom.

In this market at Locke, after we had talked a little Chinese back and forth, George Mar, who runs the meat department and who had been putting out some choice steaks for a barbecue for us, suddenly reached into the pile of steaks which was ready for wrapping, took out one which had a little oxidation on the outside, threw it back into the counter and substituted another choice steak.

"I can't sell bum steak to person who speaks good Chinese," he said by way of explanation.

On later visits we had an opportunity to get better acquainted.

The market is operated by the King familes and George Mar.

George Mar is a shrewd meat buyer as well as a skillful cutter, because the meat we secured at this market was firm, fine-grained, well colored, yet it barbecued up very tender and chock-full of juice.

Mrs. Tom King (Constance) is known throughout the community for her skill in Chinese cooking. We went back

The author and George Mar.

to this market several times, and since I have always had a feeling of warm friendship for the Chinese people I am now beginning to feel like one of the family and very much at home in this quaint Chinese city of yesterday.

The Kings' grandfather was one of the first settlers in the Community. At that time he was the only Chinese who could speak English. As a result his services were greatly in demand as an interpreter in those days when Chinese labor furnished much of the manpower.

I myself can remember those days when nearly all of these Western cities had Chinatowns and the Chinese represented a virtually unlimited reservoir of cheap labor.

Today there is hardly a Chinese in Oroville, but when I first knew it, it had a Chinatown numbering many hundreds. It had its own joss house and Chinese theater. Block after block was devoted to the little shack houses of the Chinese.

These men performed the hardest menial labor under the hottest sun, toiling unremittingly and receiving as wages only a dollar a day. They not only managed to support themselves on this money but they lived so frugally that after ten or fifteen years of this sort of work they could return to China as comparatively wealthy individuals.

We in this country are inclined to look casually upon our wonderful opportunities. We take them for granted.

In China, I have looked out over the hordes of hungry men competing to make a living, knowing — as they themselves knew — that a certain number of them were destined to starve to death during the next year. I mean literally starve to death. There simply wouldn't be enough food to go around.

When the struggle for existence gets down to such a hand-to-hand battle with starvation, it is surprising how much men can and will put up with in order to earn any kind of a living.

I think probably the whole story of Locke lies in the fact that the ranch was serviced by cheap Chinese labor; that

The World of Water

King's grandfather was probably more than an interpreter, was in fact a pretty good executive.

The Kings' father is still living today and is in his nineties, but mentally alert and very vigorous. We had a pleasant visit with him.

There are other old Chinese in Locke who can remember the past. There is one Chinese woman in her late eighties or early nineties who dates back to the era when Chinese women were supposed to have tiny feet and, in order to be sure that they had them, their feet were bound tightly with bandages so that the bones couldn't grow.

In China, I saw some of these women who could barely hobble along, women of the aristocracy who are supposed to have tiny feet, and they certainly did have tiny feet.

One of them told me of the terrific suffering that resulted from thwarting nature in this way. She felt as a child that if she could only loosen the bandages just a little it would be blissful relief.

Particularly at night the torture of the bones trying in vain to grow against the pressure of the bandages would cause excruciating agony until she felt that she simply couldn't stand it for a moment more. Yet stand it she did until her feet finally gave up the struggle and nature ceased her efforts to add to the bone structure.

It seems that the world over women will subject themselves to almost any inconvenience or actual pain in order to be in style.

Those were the days when the Chinese wore queues and it was generally believed among us Occidentals, and probably with some grounds, that a Chinese person could not return to China if his queue had been cut off.

In any event, the queue was most jealously guarded by the Chinese, and even after the edict was passed in China that the country was going modern and queues were to be cut off,

The author discusses the early history of Locke with Grandfather King and Constance King.

the Chinese population in foreign lands tenaciously hung on to their queues. It was many, many months before they could be persuaded to cut theirs off.

The most tenacious slave to the old custom, however, was the cartoonist.

When the Chinese decided to dispense with the queue, it was a body blow to many of the cartoonists. Drawing an Oriental face is not easy for many of the cartoonists, as can be seen even today, but in those days the cartoonist had an easy job. All he had to do was to make high cheekbones, slant the eyes, put on a long queue and everyone knew that he was depicting a Chinese.

When the Chinese died in this country, they were buried for a period. Then in most instances the bones were disinterred, carefully arranged in a basket and sent back to China.

It is not generally known, but there is a ritual about arranging the bones of the dead Chinese for shipment and subsequent interment in China which must be carefully complied with. The bones must be arranged in a certain pattern.

The Chinese have for centuries been bound by tradition. And always they have been shrewd bargainers.

In the Chinese kitchen is a replica of the god who presides over the destinies of the household and in particular the preparation of food.

Every year custom decrees that this god be burned so he can go to heaven and a new god put in his place.

The idea is that the burned deity goes to heaven and reports on whether the family is wasteful of foodstuffs or economical in cooking. In a country where many people are going to starve to death, the conservation of food is an important item.

It is a Chinese custom to smear the lips of the departing deity with honey before he is set afire. In that way, they feel, when he arrives in the other world his words will be sweet.

138

Mrs. King gives recipes to my secretary. Left to right: Dolores Morias (Mo's wife), the author, Constance King, and Jean Bethell.

On one occasion we took Manuel Morais (Mo) and his wife, Dolores, to Locke with us, to show us around.

Mo was raised in this community. He had gone to school with George Mar. He knew the Chinese intimately, and he knew much of the old history of Locke and many of the people.

Under his guidance we had quite a tour, renewing our acquaintanceship with the Kings and George Mar, and making an attempt to interview the aged Chinese woman with the bound feet, but she refused to come out and be interviewed.

The Kings, however, were very gracious, and Mrs. King gave my secretary, Jean Bethell, some of her secret recipes for Chinese cooking.

At one time Locke had been very wide open indeed. There

were gambling houses and there were the side alleys between buildings where the "cribs" existed.

Now all of these places are closed and drab. As King said, "This city is dying. Every day it dies a little more. There is no business to hold the young people. They leave, and the old people get older and die."

Be that as it may, Locke is one of the most picturesque cities or, if one wishes, near-ghost towns that one can find. It fairly reeks with the memories of a bygone period of our civilization.

In fact, the whole Delta country is strongly reminiscent of years gone by, years when the diesel engine, the caterpillar, paved roads, automobiles and gasoline motors were unknown.

Men toiled by the sweat of the brow. Dirt was moved by a Fresno scraper and a couple of mules, or painstakingly moved by hand, a little at a time, being placed in baskets which in turn were balanced on a bamboo pole, placed over the shoulder of some Chinese laborer and slowly and painfully transported in the hot sun.

It was a day when steamboat whistles on the river brought the communities to life, a day when living was cheap, when men were outstanding, rugged individuals, when the streets of Locke swarmed with hordes of Chinese, when the now-deserted back alleys echoed to softly seductive feminine voices.

It was a day of good, hard, sound money; a day when paper money was taboo; a day when men carried leather purses, and in those purses were five-, ten- and twenty-dollar gold pieces, while silver dollars represented the smaller denominations.

Gradually "Eastern" or paper money began to infiltrate, and for some time San Francisco would refer scornfully to paper money as "Los Angeles money."

When I first began to practice law, I never bothered

Peat fields blowing away.

keeping books. There was no income tax. I took in fees in gold coin, put the gold coin in my pocket, took it home and spent it. I didn't know how much I had made at the end of the year. I only knew how much I had left. No one else knew what I was doing; it was none of their business.

I contrast that with nowadays, when there is no such thing any more as "hard money," when I have to keep track of every dime I take in, when I not only have to make a profit but am taxed on that profit, when every dollar of expense I pay out in making that profit is subject to the scrutiny of some person who knows nothing about my individual business problems but who decides whether it was a "necessary" expense.

Then every so often a team of auditors comes down and disrupts the office for days at a time checking into every item, wanting explanations, sending the secretaries scurrying around bringing out papers on this and that, disallowing, checking, questioning.

Nowadays buying dinner for a group of business people entails vouchers, checks and cross-checks. In those days it was necessary only to pay the check, leave a tip and walk out.

If any stranger wanted to know how much money you were taking in, how much you were paying out, you'd look at him in stunned amazement. If any fortune teller had predicted the ramifications of government growth during the next five decades, he'd have been put in an asylum.

It is easier to change character than we realize. In those days men were rugged individuals. They valued their freedoms and were quick to resent any infringements.

It was a period when it would have been impossible for a condition to exist where a group of persons would stand sheeplike while a young woman was being murdered, begging the bystanders for help, or where a woman would drown while a dozen people stood on the bank a few feet distant, ignoring her cries for help.

Standing there on the streets of Locke, looking at the buildings of yesterday, thinking of the old days of the riverboats, of a hard currency, which was also a sound currency, I found myself filled with nostalgic memories.

It is easy to get that feeling of wishing to hear once more the sound of steamboat whistles, mellowed by the night fog, the pound of assertive masculine feet on board sidewalks, the music of the honky-tonks.

CHAPTER 10

The World of Water
by Helicopter

Not only am I a houseboat enthusiast and a trailer addict, but I am a helicopter fan.

I love to adventure, but as before mentioned, I have chains which keep me tied to the clock and to the calendar. I have found that the use of helicopters opens up a broad, new world of adventure and enables me to get material which would otherwise be unavailable.

Most of my helicopter adventures have been in the desert and in Baja California, that long peninsula stretching from Tijuana at the International Boundary Line down well into the tropics, a peninsula that is considerably longer than the "Boot" of Italy, a peninsula of vast, open spaces, many of which are unexplored in terms of modern knowledge and travel.

Some years ago I conceived the idea of getting a helicopter to give me a look at some of this strange country.

Filled with enthusiasm, I got in touch with various com-

143

panies which manufactured or rented helicopters. They were all eager to accommodate me, until I told them where I wanted to go, and then the excuses began to pour in.

It seemed that no one wanted to risk helicopters in Baja California.

Not only was there a problem of supplying fuel and maintenance, but the land is noted for terrific turbulences. There are areas where a man having a breakdown would not only die before he could reach any human habitation but where it would probably be years before anyone knew what had happened to him.

(As I write this, two young men who went exploring in Baja California in a pickup have been missing for some weeks.)

My friend Bob Boughton is connected with the Hiller Aircraft Corporation. When I first came in contact with him, he was in charge of export sales and, because Mexico was in his territory, he wanted to find out more about what I had in mind.

He had unlimited confidence in the performance and durability of the Hiller helicopter. He said it would go anywhere.

Bob's confidence was amply justified by subsequent developments. At one time we encountered such terrific headwinds and turbulence in Baja California that we got through one of the mountain passes literally by the skin of our teeth. Bob Boughton, who has flown all over the world and under all sorts of adverse conditions, confided afterward that it was without exception the worst turbulence he had ever encountered.

I was able to work out an arrangement with him. We explored Baja California with Hiller helicopters, and I wrote several books describing our adventures. Since then we have had a species of partnership. I call on him when I'm getting

Bob Boughton, his wife, Jill, and the author standing by one of the
latest Hiller helicopters.

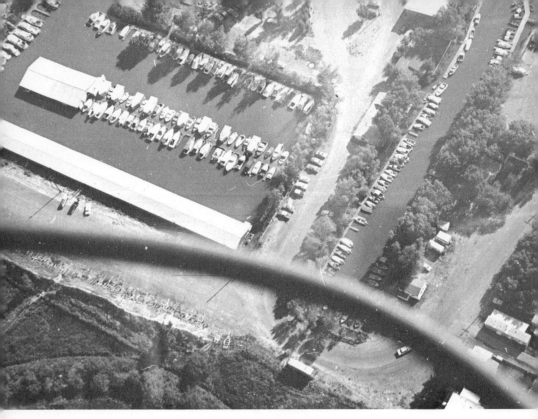

From the helicopter, I saw a world of boats.

an idea for a new adventure; he works out a deal on helicopters and a schedule — and we go exploring.

Not only have we explored Baja California but we have also covered much of the desert in California, Nevada and Arizona by helicopter. Together Bob and I have had hair-raising adventures, and we have built up a friendship based upon mutual respect and many memories.

Bob's wife, Jill, is a woman who loves action. She loves adventure, she loves flying, she loves camping, and on many of our adventures Jill has accompanied Bob, camping under conditions where there were no conveniences — and enjoying every minute of it.

So it was only natural that when I wanted to take a look at the Delta country from the air and get some aerial photographs I should call on Bob Boughton.

A fixed-wing airplane would have taken me too fast and

The Hiller over Giusti's.

too high for the pictures I wanted. A helicopter would take me where I wanted to go and could crawl along at a walk or could hover over our target. Bob got official clearance, and then called back to say that he and Jill could fly up to join us at Dick DeShazer's trailer park. (I had a field office in four house trailers parked near the docks where the house cruisers were moored.)

By the time word got around that we were going to take a look at the Delta country by helicopter, we had quite a crowd.

As it happened, Dick DeShazer was entertaining Richard and Irene Whittaker, who had flown out for a business conference. (Whittaker is the head of the Whit-Craft organization, and since I owned one of his house cruisers I was glad to include him in our party of exploration.)

It also happened that my brother, who is a medical doctor

147

My four house trailers, the first four on the upper left, at DeShazer's Trailer park.

in San Francisco, and his wife, Dorothy, had planned to visit us over the weekend.

Bob and Jill came up on a Saturday afternoon and caused quite a commotion when they landed the helicopter within walking distance of the trailer park.

Dick DeShazer had accompanied me on my explorations of the Superstition Mountains in Arizona by helicopter and had flown back from Arizona to the Delta country in a helicopter. He was, therefore, a veteran, but his wife, Moyne, had never been up in a helicopter and, enthused by Dick's description, was eager to try it.

After a few preliminary flights we tied up the helicopter and went out on one of the house cruisers, a large congenial party, yet with plenty of room for talking, lounging and, if one desired, stretching out in a berth for an afternoon siesta.

The World of Water by Helicopter

Bob, who had been working hard, had a chance to relax. Jill had brought one of her famous cheesecakes, and since it was a perfect day we enjoyed the Delta country to the utmost, returning to have a big dinner at Irving Podre's Bel-Isle Club.

The next morning we started out in earnest to do a job. We flew down to the airport at Antioch to fill the helicopter's tank with gasoline and then back to the trailers.

This latest model Hiller helicopter is a beauty, a veritable greyhound of the skies. It seems to jump up off the ground — an eager, willing machine that wants to go places. I had the feeling it was straining at the leash.

I have done quite a bit of helicoptering, but I have never before experienced such maneuverability, if one can use that word.

Left to right: Richard Whittaker, the author, and Mrs. Whittaker.

The World of Water

Bob Boughton, Dick DeShazer and I flew up over the Delta country to Giusti's.

That flight was most illuminating.

From the ground level, or perhaps I should say from the water level, one sees the winding channel and the high levees; but from the helicopter one sees thousands of acres of fertile land crowded with crops, channels filled with boats.

We flew over a tomato field where the laborers were busy picking tomatoes, great, luscious, vine-ripened red tomatoes which filled box after box down the long rows of vines.

In fact, the fertility of this land as seen from the air is one of the most amazing things about it.

While we were flying up to Giusti's in the helicopter, the others were coming by automobiles to join us.

Wave patterns made by a speeding boat, as seen from the helicopter.

Doris Waterworth, the author, and Jean Bethell.

Water skier from the air.

We landed in a field just back of Giusti's and took up Mo and Lo to give them a look at the Delta country.

We had promised Mr. and Mrs. Waterworth that we would show them their ranch from the air. The Waterworths own some of the property directly across from where we had tied up our house cruisers on those never-to-be-forgotten lazy days while we were relaxing, swimming, fishing and taking photographs.

Unfortunately, Jerry Waterworth was involved in a business deal from which he couldn't get away, but Doris Waterworth came, and we took her for a flight over the lagoon and over her ranch so that she could see it from the air.

By that time the others had arrived in the automobiles, and we buckled down to work in earnest.

We wanted pictures of various types of boats in action, and we wanted pictures of water skiers.

The World of Water by Helicopter

Photographing a water skier from a helicopter presents some difficulties. The ordinary slow-speed water skier doesn't present dramatic photographic material when seen from a helicopter. On the other hand, the high-speed ski artist presents something of a problem.

If he is moving fast enough to make a really dramatic shot from a helicopter, he is going at such speed that a spill might be injurious, and a helicopter at high speed makes quite a current of air and also furnishes a potentially diastrous distraction.

A man who is an amateur at skiing, keeping his balance while going at high speed, hearing a sudden roar above his head while a shadow passes over him accompanied by a blast of air, might look up in panic, lose his balance and take a bad tumble.

However, we found two or three skiers who were so skillful that they took us in their stride, and we found one skier who

Skiing along at a fast clip.

was clipping along over the water at between fifty-five and sixty miles an hour.

We got just a few feet over his head and to one side, and I took a series of photographs, much to the apparent delight of the man, who was really a superb performer.

I could hardly believe my eyes when we checked the air speed indicator on the helicopter and found the rate at which this boat was skimming over the water with the skier sweeping along behind in a series of graceful maneuvers.

By this time we had taken the two doors off the helicopter so that we could photograph without being bothered by the reflections of the plastic bubble, and I confess it was a little scary.

I was a rather snug fit; in fact, it really takes the closed door of a helicopter to keep all of me in the machine.

As Mo said when he was standing on the ground helping me adjust the seat belt before the flight, "It's that guy in the middle that keeps pushing you out, Erle."

The seat belt was supposed to hold me in, and of course I could help by hanging on with my fingers, but when I had to manipulate the camera with both hands, turning half sideways, straining against the seat belt, I could only hope that no sudden maneuvers would be necessary.

It was just as we were getting some good pictures of this skier that Bob Boughton's keen eyes detected a couple of telephone wires strung across the slough at just about the height we were flying and directly ahead of us.

Bob has about the fastest reactions of any pilot I know, and they certainly came in good stead at this time.

Seen from above, the surface of the water was dark in color, the telephone wires were dark, there was nothing in the way of a warning and we were right on top of those wires before we could see them.

Bob took that machine up in the air so fast that I felt my

The Meadows from the air.

head settle down until my ears seemed to be resting on my shoulders. But we missed the wires.

After that we photographed Locke from the air, then we went up in The Meadows and flew along over the water, looking at the various cruisers and taking photographs of the family parties picnicking along the beach.

It was a splendid sight from the air, and not only did we enjoy it but the various yachtsmen came out on deck to wave at us and seemed to get as big a kick out of it as we did.

It must have seemed quite a spectacle to these yachtsmen to have a helicopter flying eighty or ninety miles an hour about twenty feet off the surface of the water, skimming along smoothly, with both doors off and a bulky passenger bulging out to the side, holding a camera in both hands with only a straining seat belt keeping him in position.

155

The World of Water

Bob made several trips up over The Meadows with different members of the group so that we could get a good survey of the place.

He also made some trips over Locke, but there are some natural hazards around Locke which make it advisable to keep rather high. A television relay tower, as seemingly slender as a lead pencil, thrusts its way up into the sky fifteen hundred and forty-nine feet. It is, of course, anchored in place with huge guy wires stretching around in a circle.

This tower is just outside of Locke, and I had warned Bob about it and suggested that we keep our distance and our elevation. Hitting one of those wires could have wrecked not only our plans but also our helicopter and our futures.

Shortly after lunch we had completed our photographic assignments over The Meadows and Snodgrass Slough and were ready to start back. Bob couldn't resist the temptation to take another type of ride, so he hitchhiked a ride on an opening drawbridge.

There was a big picnic gathering at one of the resorts on the river, and Dick DeShazer had sent up both a River Queen and a Whit-Craft. He thought it would be a good thing to get photographs of the helicopter hovering over these boats, and I wanted to get some pictures from the air showing the performance of the boats.

We gave Dick a head start so he could get on the job, and after we had allowed him time to get in position Sam and I climbed in the helicopter with Bob Boughton and we took off.

By the time we arrived, Dick had his boats out in the middle of the stream, and not only were we able to get some pictures of them from the air, but Bob Boughton was able to put the helicopter almost on top of the boats so that Dick could get some interesting shots from the shore.

156

We flew by a group of houseboats at high speed.

Locke from aloft.

Bob Boughton hitches a ride on an opening drawbridge.

When we had finished with those pictures, we bounced up in the air again and made a beeline for the Antioch airfield, as we were beginning to be short of gas.

We filled up, and the Boughtons took off for home, gliding over the congested Sunday traffic in a smooth, graceful flight which made the helicopter nothing but a dot in the sky within a matter of seconds after the take-off.

These new Hiller helicopters are really a dream. They circle and hover, descend as gently as a bird and take off with smooth efficiency.

The World of Water is a wonderful world indeed.

There is something soothing and relaxing about water. Apparently there is a layer of fresh, oxygen-saturated air clinging to the surface of the water which gives one an appetite during the day and is conducive to sound slumber at night.

158

The World of Water by Helicopter

On that Saturday afternoon we had eleven people on our house cruiser with ample seating capacity for everyone, with no one getting in another's way, with plenty of stove space for hot coffee and refrigerator space for hors d'oeuvres. There was also plenty of locker space for drinks, and a relaxing, informal companionship which made for an enjoyable afternoon.

Traffic around the big cities has become so heavy that it is difficult to find relaxation with an automobile. The

View from the helicopter shows how the Whit-Craft lifts up in front and skims over the water.

The River Queen.

day of the enjoyable Sunday drive is, in too many instances, a thing of the past.

But there are waterways within reach of many of the cities where a person can have a boat which he can reach on a Friday night, when there is comparatively little traffic, where he can spend the night in snug contentment, cruise on Saturday and Sunday, arise early Monday morning and be back at the office fresh as a morning dewdrop.

The World of Water is filled with adventure, relaxation and friendship. It is truly a wonderful world.